Some Kids Are Blind

by Lola M. Schaefer

Consulting Editor: Gail Saunders-Smith, Ph.D.

Consultant: Dr. Marc Maurer, President
National Federation of the Blind

Pebble Books

an imprint of Capstone Press
Mankato, Minnesota

Pebble Books are published by Capstone Press
151 Good Counsel Drive, P.O. Box 669, Mankato, Minnesota 56002
http://www.capstone-press.com

1 2 3 4 5 6 06 05 04 03 02 01

Library of Congress Cataloging-in-Publication Data
Schaefer, Lola M., 1950–
    Some kids are blind/by Lola M.Schaefer.
    p. cm.—(Understanding differences)
    Includes bibliographical references and index.
    Summary: Simple text and photographs describe children who are blind, their
challenges and adaptations, and their everyday activities.
    ISBN 0-7368-0664-4
    1. Blind—Juvenile literature. [1. Blind. 2. Physically handicapped.] I. Title.
II. Series.
HV1593. S28 2001
362.4′0973—dc21

00-027708

Note to Parents and Teachers

The Understanding Differences series supports national social studies standards related to individual development and identity. This book describes children who are blind and illustrates their special needs. The photographs support early readers in understanding the text. The repetition of words and phrases helps early readers learn new words. This book also introduces early readers to subject-specific vocabulary words, which are defined in the Words to Know section. Early readers may need assistance to read some words and to use the Table of Contents, Words to Know, Read More, Internet Sites, and Index/Word List sections of the book.

Table of Contents

4

Some kids are blind. Kids who are blind cannot see.

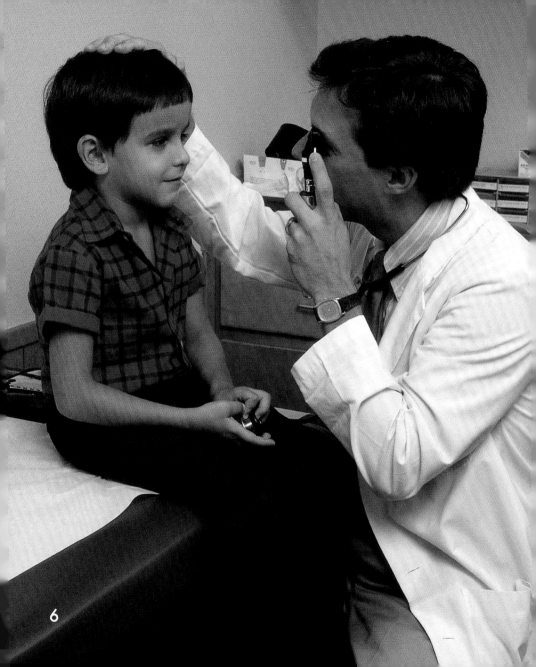

Some kids are blind
when they are born.
Some kids become
blind from a sickness
or from getting hurt.

Kids who are blind depend more on their other senses. They use their ears to listen. They use their hands to feel.

Some kids who are blind read Braille. Braille is print made of raised dots. The dots stand for letters and numbers.

Kids who are blind can tell time. They use Braille watches or talking clocks.

Some people who are blind use canes to guide them. Adults who are blind can use dog guides.

Some kids who are blind enjoy art classes.

Some kids who are blind use Braille keyboards to write.

Some kids who are blind
ride bikes. They like
to have fun.

Words to Know

blind—unable to see or having very limited sight; there are varying degrees of blindness; some people who are blind can see light and color.

Braille—a set of raised dots that stand for letters and numbers; people use their fingertips to read the raised dots; Louis Braille of France invented Braille in the early 1800s.

dog guide—a dog that is specially trained to lead adults who are blind; dog guides help adults who are blind move safely in public places.

keyboard—the set of keys on a computer or typewriter

senses—ways of learning about your surroundings; hearing, smelling, touching, tasting, and sight are the five senses.

Read More

Schulman, Arlene. *T.J.'s Story: A Book about a Boy Who Is Blind.* Minneapolis: Lerner Publications, 1998.

Westcott, Patsy. *Living with Blindness.* Austin, Texas: Raintree Steck-Vaughn, 1999.

White, Peter. *Being Blind.* Think About. Mankato, Minn.: Smart Apple Media, 1999.

Internet Sites

Blindness Resource Center
http://www.nyise.org/blind.htm

Canadian National Institute for the Blind
http://www.cnib.ca

National Federation of the Blind
http://www.nfb.org

Index/Word List

art, 17
bikes, 21
Braille, 11,
  13, 19
canes, 15
clocks, 13
dog guides,
  15

dots, 11
feel, 9
guide, 15
hurt, 7
keyboards, 19
letters, 11
listen, 9
numbers, 11

print, 11
ride, 21
see, 5
senses, 9
sickness, 7
time, 13
watches, 13

Word Count: 134
Early-Intervention Level: 9

Editorial Credits
Mari C. Schuh, editor; Kia Bielke, designer; Katy Kudela, photo researcher

Photo Credits
Daemmrich/Pictor, 6
Gregg R. Andersen, cover, 12, 16, 18, 20
National Federation of the Blind, 1, 4
PhotoDisc, Inc., 8, 10, 14 (top)
The Seeing Eye, 14 (bottom)

Special thanks to the students and staff at the Minnesota State Academy for the Blind in Faribault, Minnesota, for their assistance with this book.